HIDDEN

By

Jonathan Christopher

JONATHAN CHRISTOPHER

ISBN: 978-1515235934
ISBN-10: 1515235939:

<u>Dedication</u>

For all those that suffer from mental illness in paralyzing isolation. Please ask someone for a pen instead of a gun. And for Betty Jones whose walls were covered in a language only understood by angels, and yes Betty, the Father.

HIDDEN

Table of Contents
Chapter 1 – Gifts

Chapter 2 – Illusion

Chapter 3 – Hidden

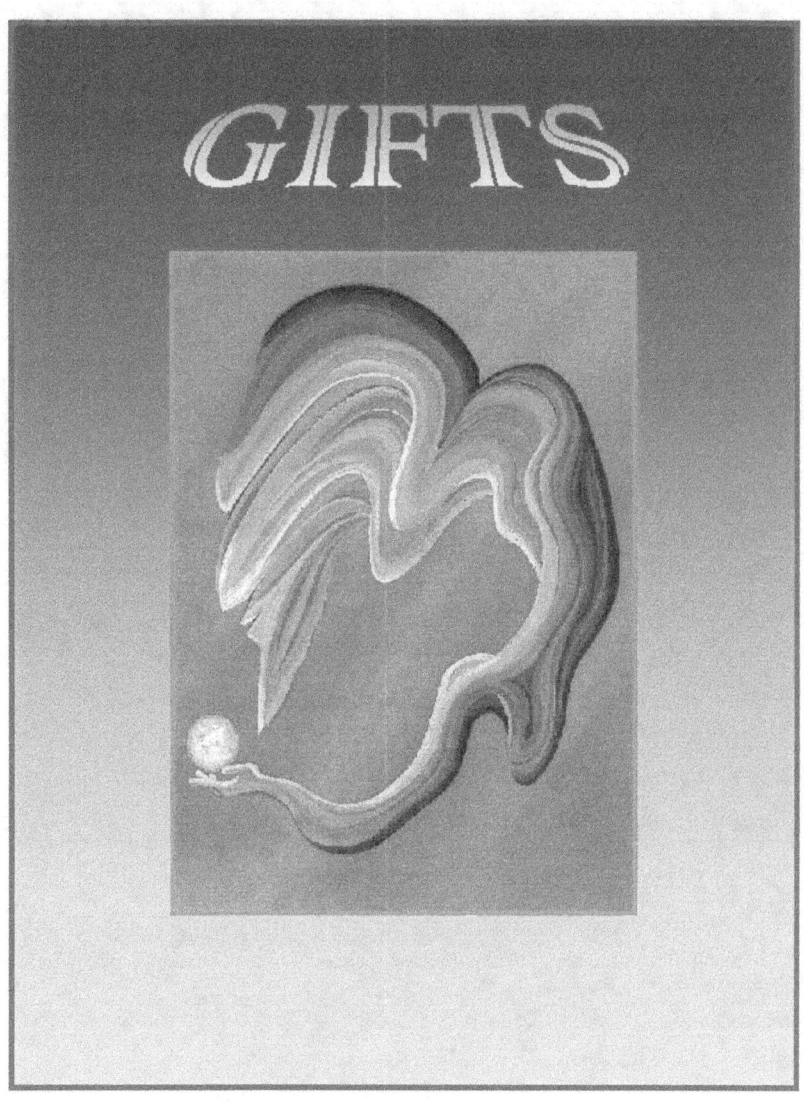

GIFTS

The Gifts of Youth

We stood on drops of Sun as proud guards of the sky.
Our hearts wove an amber meadow and fresh air into our eyes.
Our bones were bells that chimed in a playful breeze.
We spun the Earth with our feet,
and pulled the Sun through our cheeks.
We knew why the wind rose against the Sun,
Why the Moon split in two,
And why the Stars pricked in our veins.

Autumn Celebration

Luminous yellow, blazing red,
And deep rusty leaves
Permeate a sprawling forest.
The colorful and faded leaves
Fold and curl,
Twist and turn,
Chatter and break.
A breathtaking chill
Carries these summer dreams
Into the air,
And a mesmerizing ballet ensues
In a crisp blue autumn sky.
Across the fine blue
Dark and fiery leaves
Dance slowly and wildly
In circles, spirals, and lines;
Over and under straight or bent arms of wood.
A hush and rush flows through the forest
Blowing sweet perfume
Into a spinning celebration
Absent of hesitation or attachment.

9

Sacred Hymns

I prefer the timeless horizon
And the boundless sanctuary.
I prefer sacred hymns
Of nameless spheres.
I prefer the organic pendulum
That compels us to live
Beyond the anatomy of the universe.

Light and Attentive

We are light and attentive
Watching each others eye
Breaking in spacious beats
A trumpet blast of smiles
It is a pleasure to be in your presence
It is a pleasure to serve you

A Gift

Just a simple gift
Buried with thousands like this
Currents of air burst from your lips
Buried with thousands like this
Look at all these paper clams
That have murmured
Thousands like this...
For you a simple gift

One Envelope

One envelope sleeps in a bag full of gems
A myriad of color glimmers over and around
This peaceful paper clam
Now a torrent of whispers slide inside that bag,
And a deliberate wind makes it so
Alluring gems and a quiet little clam
Ride on the currents of tired legs and sore feet
But some bellies are full and some songs are heard
It may be soon or never

To Eden

Your passion is an inviting melody that fills the room.
Your enchanting essence lures me from a slumber
With energizing fervor
Cumbrous anxiety dissolves
And warm waves pulsate under my chest
Suddenly something happens that I do not expect
Your clear brown eyes allow me freedom
To go here or there
Anywhere within the vast ocean that is your eye

Lenora

Lenora is a heavenly secret.
The lustrous gems of the midnight sky
Flicker and flash,
Shimmer and shine
Like the blaze that churns in her eyes.
And just as that dark blanket sown with diamonds
Captivates those that search its beauty,
So does Lenora captivate my heart.

Lenora's eyes are brilliant passage ways
That stretch across the eons.
They stir an ancient desire within me,
But the age of that desire
Does not exceed the infinite calm
Of letting go.

A Simple Choice

Light and energy pulsed through the night
Delighted voices boomed beyond sight
The air was filled with perfumes and food
I lay on my back and loved the mood
I listened with pleasure to your voice
And ruminated over a choice
Should I stay and listen from this tomb
Or join the party in the next room

But I mulled over this decision
With little power or precision
Because reason replaced emotion
And slowly displaced my devotion

The tiny room I was twisted in
Had become even lower and thin
Those thrilled voices that flowed through our place
Vexed me and sent heat into my face

Then I realized your voice had gone
I listened as our guests carried on
But had not heard your familiar sound
Many minutes passed before I found
The gift of your unique laugh and voice
Quickly I rose with a simple choice

Muse of Inspiration

You are a shimmering light in an endless sky.
Your voice more soothing than the whisper of a distant sea.
Your eyes are a vigorous flame.
Your elegant smile pursues me even in the world of dreams.
Your laughter is a blessing I delight in.
Your kiss a moment I remember again and again.
When night and day is an ordeal
You are the calm between the two.

Smitten

Your alluring spirit and radiating energy is startling.
You are an enigmatic light in a dark forest.
Your warmth is engulfing and potent.
You are a mesmerizing flame dancing victoriously.

Memory

The currents of winter spill relentlessly across this icy shore,
But a warm whisper resonates as music on this fluttering door.
Breath quivers till still, heart stumbles till stop,
Dancing flame evens from bottom to top.
Motionless on icy shore - warm brilliant light
Floods an empty soul comfort this long cold night.

ILLUSION

An Image of a Forest

It is a frigid January midnight in a dense forest. Heavy snow embraces the bare wood and frozen earth like a lost child finally found. The light from a waxing gibbous moon and scattered stars slightly illuminate the land. The gentle touch of moonlight and blinking stars weaves a subtle shade of blue upon the snow and twisting frames of trees. When the wind moves through the forest branches they appear then vanish in the mild moonlight. The slow sway of tree limbs is hypnotic. It is as if the trees are inviting me to quiet my mind. The thought of altruistic trees is amusing and adds a little warmth to my body. I take a deep breath then lean against a poplar tree with my left shoulder. Several minutes pass as my gaze slowly drifts back and forth from the forest to the moon. I feel at ease and safe among the sleeping wood.

But soon my mood darkens and I find myself staring blankly. The enchantment of the forest is gone. I feel cold and embarrassed. I lift myself away from the poplar tree and straighten my back. Then I slowly walk past the dormant trees and exit the forest.

Lone Wolf

Gone astray from within
Looking for a place to rest
Intent on Heaven
And may not find Earth
The hour seems so far away
Yet could be knocking
Roads lead in every direction
And hesitation accompanies them
The Sun hasn't arrived yet
And the Moon glows somewhere
While I slip into the night

Oblivion

Streets, sidewalks, and alleyways weave and shake in my eyes.
The pavement bends and springs under my feet.
Dizzying distortions in space and form divert my attention
From the melancholy that brought me to this place.
Vivid neon and argon signs line the streets
Like fiery flowers that thrust aside the darkness.
Cheer and laughter tumbles through the air
From tavern to street and street to tavern.
Everyone appears jovial and kind.
But the night has just begun.
Vexations and expectations have not mingled long enough
For the fabric of our hearts to erode.
I've wandered this way many times.
There is always sorrow by nights end.
But not yet!
The night is young,
And I'm drunker than I've ever been.
When the sorrow arrives
I won't recognize it.
I won't recognize much of anything.

The Little Room

A terrific pleasure extends ominously through my body
There is wine at the table and madness in my eye
I plot to find the hero
And confront a pandemonium at the door
But I am a foggy glass
Filled with the Devil's blood
Instead, I will stare stupidly
Within a little room
And devour time
There is no one at the door

An Elusive Agent

There is an elusive agent living within me
A parasitical consciousness or toxic chemical
When it meddles with my brain
An emotional collapse devours my eyes

I lose reason,
Dignity,
And consolation
I am a burden,
A fool,
A mystery,
And a portal to Hell

Schizoaffective

Something sinister that splits the brain.
A catastrophe that cages care, confounds, and dissects dreams.
Both paranoia and obsession are mingled so perversely
That a grotesque calamity maybe seconds from fruition.
When the malady pulls my veins and arteries with a violent jerk,
It's time to avert a tragedy and retreat.

Ghoulish games and thunderous thoughts
Devils, demons, tricksters, and treachery
A grand labyrinth that stretches from one worry to the next
An effective prison
An arena of absurdity
A bastion constantly beset

Wonderful Silence

How does that trickster open the gate?
How does that diabolical creature climb into my head?

Why does such depravity haunt me?
This level of pain is more than I can bear.

This predicament shouldn't even exist!
Go! Leave me! Be gone!

Your voice is a pebble beneath a crashing wave!
Your existence agitated to a part-less powder!

A Devil's Gruel

A long fight with a devil
Can mangle and dishevel
Any person's appearance
Or shake a just adherence
To that which is true and good
Tis doubt that is the firewood
It is the cause of despair
A calamitous affair
That can sever hope in half
And stir a devil to laugh
Doubt is a devil's gruel
It's where evil draws fuel

Temptation

A broad unrestrained desire
Challenges me with ferocious zeal
An abyss spins in my eye
And opens the locked door
A jagged precipice mocks my will
And a monster calls my name

The Cloudy Window

Lust is a cloudy window
Set in a decrepit house
The moment I desire this view
Space narrows
And the window appears before me
When I peer out the hazy glass
Space narrows again
And darkness surrounds me

Hideous specters weave themselves into the fabric
Of the darkness
They move in such a way
That I become hypnotized
And distant
A cold thing
Falling dead

Burial Place in Autumn

Here lies an open grave
Cold, wet, and foul
A miserable moment to ponder
An undesired darkness to curl inside
The only companions to console me at this grave
Are the aged oaks and the stubborn rusty leaves
That clings to its arms
The leaves flutter and wave
Hello, good-bye, hello, good-bye
This is the first night I am with you
Because I lost you alive
And I found you dead

Unforeseen

Saturn choked me
And I climbed oh so high, oh so still
And this was day
A fiery furnace that plunged in my eye
A ferocious spectacle of vivid gore
Deprived of my throat
I winced and shook
But Saturn thumbed his way deep
Oh so hard, oh so still
The might of harvest was too much to bear
All I could do was stare, stare, stare...

A Brief Hope

Occasionally, brief moments of clarity surface
And a world previously unknown is revealed
When this happens I am stricken with awe
Endless possibilities lay before me
Mountains of discontent evaporate
Optimism flourishes in the air
A maelstrom of emotion seizes my throat
My heart explodes wide and warm
A melody rises through my arteries
And slips out the corner of my eyes
Yet just as sudden as the lucidity arose
A great noise violently charges in

Recurring Storm

A storm below a mountain rages
Senses churn through a valley
Vices grind beside a mountain
Rhythm quickly rises then slowly dies
Night pursues a day
Mind chases a shadow
Light leaps away
The Sun bitten by a mountain

An Ancient Fear

There is an ancient fear
That I have not been able to overcome
It is a potent desperate fear
That chains me to a small dark room

Sometimes I wake from sleep terrified
Terrified of my breath
Terrified of the body that holds me hostage
To this world and realm

Perhaps because I've been born
Countless times
Perhaps because I've been hunted
Countless times
Perhaps because I've been imprisoned
Countless times
Perhaps because I've been executed
Countless times
Countless times
Countless times

HIDDEN

Amidst the Desolate

A fierce winter current rages through wide gaps between tall twisted trees. High gray clouds stretch across the sky from horizon to horizon. The turbulent air strips variation from the cloud cover. It is plain and distant. The sunlight is so diffuse that the landscape appears dull and remote. Even the recent layer of snow that clings to this park has lost its luster.

What is more disconcerting is the frigid blast of air that not only persuades wildlife to seek refuge, but me as well. The conditions are simply too unpleasant for me to continue walking through the park. I bring my jacket closer to my body, take a deep breath, and walk away from the park.

Suddenly there is movement in the periphery of my sight. I turn, but there is nothing in that vicinity. Nevertheless, curiosity compels me to wander in that direction. However, as I close the distance between me and the edge of the park it becomes clear that there is no mystery. There's nothing to be found. I change direction, but as I do something startles me. A dark figure sits on a park bench right in front of me. I blink a few times and squint to see if my eyes deceive me. Yet they do not. *Why did I not see this figure on my approach? Have I lost my mind? What sort of perverse illusion challenges my vision? Am I dreaming?* Unsure of my bearings, I address the figure.

"Hello?" I cautiously utter, but there is no response.

The dark figure is that of a middle-aged woman dressed in black. I stand about twenty feet to her left. She faces the icy Mississippi River at just the right angle for me to remain unnoticed. Her countenance is peculiar. She seems oblivious to the harsh weather. Her wool coat is open, and her posture is relaxed. What is more interesting is her facial expression, but it is the only eye that I can see that really intrigues me. My interest is so powerful that I suddenly find myself eight or ten feet from her. Feelings of embarrassment are thrust aside for foolish fascination.

The complexity within this woman's eye is extraordinary. It's difficult for me to unravel. Her eye radiates mystery, color, and light so fiercely that the environment is comfortably cool and vibrant. Brilliant and startling color shimmers around her pupil like many tiny gems. The variation in color is impossible. Sometimes her eye flashes like stunning aquamarine, then pale jade, then deep and rich onyx.

Her pale face glows just as bright as her eye, however her expression is inscrutable. *What is she thinking? What stills this woman, and vexes me so effectively?*

Slowly her composure changes. She tightens a bit. Her gaze falls and she gently rises from the park bench. The entire time her eyes are lowered.

Embarrassment holds me still as the woman leaves the edge of my vision. I simply stand there head bent low. The seconds pass agonizingly slow as I wait until I am certain she is a good distance from me before I move. I don't want to intrude upon her privacy any more than I already have. As I stand there the complete significance of the experience occurs to me. I recall the restlessness that wrenched me from a warm apartment and pushed me into a cold empty park. I recall the sadness that mercilessly stung my heart as I walked two miles through subzero temperatures. I recall the dreadful disappointment of a lifeless park. And I recall the unpleasant decision to turn back unfulfilled. But there is one thing I am unable to recall because I had accepted the idea that I was hopelessly unique.

The weight of my delusion only increases as I draw her image from my memory. I swallow hard and spin around to catch a glimpse of the woman one last time—She is gone. I turn here and there, but there is no sign of her. There is no sign of anyone. I try to picture her eye again to retrieve that one thing I so carelessly ignored. That one question that might diminish this melancholy which grips me so ferociously. *What brought **her** to this cold empty park?*

Interference

I explore the space within
To find the treasures therein.

I focus my willpower
For a minute then an hour.

Thoughts pull me away then close
To that great inner cosmos.

Yet dysfunction in my brain
Twists the desire to sustain

A search for inner treasure.
I want an instant pleasure.

Caught in a Snare

A tiny virtuous fire
Is swallowed by a great mire.
All things familiar are lost;
A wild place I have been tossed.

I sink in an ugly muck.
A rank soup I glumly suck.
The stench pulls my lips to frown.
I vomit then breathe to drown.
Yet I survive this affair,
And this adds to my despair.
I search the pestilent glue,
And see movement in the stew.
Odd creatures gurgle and moan,
Snort and spit this hell our own.
Their forms are long, thin, and pale;
Some are human, mostly male.
The others flat sickly forms
That convulse in giant swarms.
I look more and am aghast
At the countless numbers cast
Into this vile sea of grief
That's taken us like a thief.
Desperation ends my shock
As pus clumps once more to block
The entry to my windpipe.
This pain is a nasty type.
For I suffocate and live.
This sad sea steals all I give.
Suddenly the fetid paste
Confronts my will to make haste,
And find release from its grasp
That tightens with every gasp.

HIDDEN

But no matter where I hunt
The outcome is bleak and blunt.
No one is able to aid.
Because all seek to evade
This cocktail of epic pain
That suffocates us so plain.

But this ghastly state must end!
Yes! My life I won't defend.

With this thought I slowly slip
Then fall at a dreadful clip.
The murky mess splits apart,
And I descend like a dart
Flung hard into an abyss.
Sludge hurtles by with a hiss
Till there's no scrap within view;
Dark empty space I fall through.

The air is cold and I wet.
Remnants of the mire are set
Upon my bare skin like gum.
I grow colder and am glum
As I fall ever so fast
Through this dark realm that is vast.

My descent endures too long.
My weak mind skips and jerks wrong.
Strange beings with bulbous eyes
Appear then vanish with cries.
My mind screws tightly manic.
I laugh out of sheer panic.

Faster and faster I fall
Then I snap and loudly bawl.
White light cleaves the dismal space
As I wail and gouge my face.

But the plunge continues on
Amidst this bright ugly dawn.
I laugh uproariously.
This is home gloriously!
But giddy insanity
Contains bits of vanity.
Time wears that away quickly,
And again I feel sickly.
Curse this desolate decline
Along this vertical line!

Strangely I lose my vile form.
Then gain the sense I am warm.
Orange hue pervades the air
That appears quite still and fair.

This is a welcome release
For such lunacy to cease;
An exultant spacious calm
An eloquent silent psalm.
I feel so immensely free
To have cast off the body.

Yet as I grow more content
A noise stirs somewhere distant.

What is this elusive din
That shrinks this space I am in?

Soon the distant sound grows clear
As an image does appear.
The sight and sound is a shock;
A vision I cannot block.
A perverse version of me
Howls and glares bold mockery.
He or it continues on.
I wish the image were gone.

HIDDEN

This cruel act stings deeply;
An absurd facsimile.

The performance grows in pace
When this thing tears at its face.
My loathsome copy bleeds fast
When flesh is hastily cast.
The ugly work shows no bone.
Instead a new face is shown.
The face of a bat and ape
Merge to form a bizarre shape.
On top its head are small ears
That look like the tips of spears.
The things nose is broad and flat.
Its lips thin and its jaw fat.
But its eyes hold all the fright.
They're small glassy orbs of night.

Now with a violent shake
The surface body parts break,
And fall away to reveal
A creature very surreal.

It is a muscular mass
That appears like tarnished brass.
Its legs are like thick oak trunks.
Its arms are large meaty hunks.
Its chest is quite wide and dense.
Its belly round and immense.
The mammoth thing gives a grin
That draws out its teeth therein.
Suddenly the beast explodes;
Pieces hurl in heavy loads.
Orange space changes to black,
And the body I did lack
Returns complete with sharp pain.
This torture is too much strain.

I long for liberation;
An end to this frustration.
Abruptly a warm voice booms.

"Creatures drown in murky tombs.
Think of how suffering looms
For these countless sad life forms
Who toss and turn in Hell's storms."

The booming voice troubles me.
I scan dark space nervously.
What does this speaker imply;
When my pain does multiply?
The voice returns calm and plain.

"I am here to ease your pain."

What sort of being is this
To understand without miss?
I muster my strength to speak
To find the cure that I seek,
But the being interjects.

"Find where your pain intersects
With countless suffering lives.
You will know where pain derives.
Yet beware of that creature
That masquerades as teacher."

- With those last words wind flows by,
And hope fills the clear black sky.

Invasion and Panic

Wonderment leapt from my heart.
Swiftly demons crushed that art
That spun free above my chest.
The winds within fought this test
With furious confusion
At this sudden intrusion.
The water that cupped my eyes
Rose into uncertain skies.
My pupils drifted away,
And burned up in the noonday.
Something foul leaked from my pores
As one ill deed turned to scores.
So I clawed at bars of soap,
And added water for hope.
But my hands were never clean,
Not with one wash or thirteen.
I washed only to be cursed.
A great filth I was immersed.
I wallowed in self-pity,
And hid within a city.
Life stirred beyond a dark glass.
Locals strode the streets en masse.
Their energetic movement
Urged me to make improvement.
So I decided to leave
The home behind on the eve
Of glorious redemption.
Fate had offered preemption.

But demon clamor froze me.
I was as still as a tree.
I backed away from the door,
And climbed the steps to my floor.

I felt like I was on a ship
That pitched and rolled ready to tip.
I gasped for air and clutched the walls.
Thick smog poked and burned my eyeballs.
I opened my mouth and grunted.
My head swelled and thoughts were stunted.
I hummed a ridiculous tune,
And prayed this chaos would end soon.

And when I reached that final brick
That harsh gale couldn't bend a stick.

Something Stirs Among the Pine

Trees don't coordinate a hunt,
Nor do they uproot to confront.
Trees don't have eyelids or a lens.
Dark insects bunch in threes or tens.
Trees do not cackle, whine, or groan.
Close trees may lean and cause a tone.
Trees do not whisper a warning.
Wind may blow noon, night, and morning.

Yet something stirs among the pine.
A presence that I can't divine.
It feels like eyes are upon me;
An old gaze pressing its decree.
But I understand illusion.
Am I caught in a delusion?

If I am the truth can't be known.
   These ideas flimsily sown.
But I won't let this rest so quick.
This sense is real and not a trick.
Something does stir among the pine.
   It is not dark nor does it shine.
Sometimes I feel it above me;
Other times behind the next tree.
   At times I feel its stare behind.
Then feel a sharp sense it's not kind.
I confront the phantom and turn.
Yet there's only the pine and fern.
   Am I mad or am I the prey?
What thing causes me such dismay?

Phantasmal—Grotesque

Something is attached to my face.
   It's a nauseating disgrace.

Yet there are times I'm unaware,
And moments that I need not care
About the odd thing that protrudes
Out my head and face and intrudes
Upon my sense of contentment.
It's nature that treats the torment.

The many trees I walk among
Are bent or twisted old and young.
Some have huge growths that slowly weep,
And others have wounds very deep.
But some of these scarred trees persist
Even those with a gaping cyst.

It's healing to wander alone,
And rest on a large rugged stone.
Then watch nature whirl, dash, and sway;
Absorb that which words can't convey,
Breathe the magnificent fresh air,
And be still in this land I share.

Yes others walk this treasured land.
They traverse narrow paths of sand.
I allow them space and respect,
And hope they don't see my defect.
But almost every time they do -
To see them recoil is not new.

What deformity do they see?
My hands find no anomaly.

Even so, there is something there.
Since childhood I have been aware
Of a phantom malformation,
But have not found its causation.

Times of Old

I want to know the beings of legend and myth.
Back when men carved and moved by hand a megalith.
I want to understand that sacred alignment,
And how holy beings advised the assignment.
I want a fair view of the supernatural
Before the legends and myths became scriptural.
I want to eliminate my ego and fear,
And meticulously draw the times of old near.

Hidden

Bitter wind arrives from the north.
A dense group of dark clouds come forth.
There's a palpable urgency,
And a peculiar pungency
That saturates the air and earth.
Creatures dart and flee from its girth.

A sultry southern wind merges
With the frigid northern surges.
The strength of sunlight decreases
As the mass of cloud increases.
The sky turns a dark rusty hue
That stains everything within view.

Several spears of lightning flash.
Electric charges split and clash.
Drifting mist becomes heavy rain.
Soon a torrent fills the terrain.
Great sturdy trees contort and tear.
Leaves, wood, and sand turn in the air.
The wild currents create a sound
Like a piercing grind all around.
Quickly there's nothing to discern.
All is hidden in the fierce turn
Of raging wind flows and matter,
Even notions of self scatter.

A Luminous Day

The sky was the brightest and clearest blue I'd ever seen.
I stared into that endless expanse that glowed so pristine,
And experienced an ethereal calm and wholeness.
That was the summer my eyes were filled with light and boldness.

Every person that I saw in the park that day shed light.
Some of the people smiled, many laughed, and some were uptight.
But even those that displayed dejection upon their face
Could neither hide nor extinguish their radiance and grace.

All of this happened long ago.
When I was two and did not know
Of hate and the other dark things
That has murdered peasants and kings.

Joseph Merrick

I'm hidden inside a mountain;
A spacious cave with a fountain.
There is no need for a candle.
There's room for a child to dandle.
Besides I'm the light in this cave.
Light flows from my heart to my eye.
Vigilance and patience I brave,
And I will do so till I die.

Father—Mother Sky

I tripped and tumbled to the ground.
Small new bones hardly made a sound,
In that voluminous new world,
Which swallowed me as I curled.
Swiftly you scooped me from terror,
And loved me despite my error.

Now the decades have come and gone;
Time stretched as long as an eon.
The wide sky is my father now,
For in this large womb I shall bow.

The Beginning

You are a splendid musician
A spectacular magician
When this heart is ragged and cold
You still offer shimmering gold
An amber spark cracking the dark
A soothing wind striking its mark
You quell the desire to give up
Thank you for filling this small cup

About the Author

Jonathan Christopher lives in West Central Wisconsin. He lives with the diagnosis schizoaffective by channeling his energy through creative means such as: writing, painting, and composing music. He enjoys hiking through the forests that cover the gentle rolling coulees of West Central Wisconsin.

www.ingramcontent.com/pod-product-compliance
Lightning Source LLC
Chambersburg PA
CBHW070349290526
45791CB00003B/1490